To Woody....who has shown me the meaning of "courage," "determination" and "love."

Even though Woody had always been blind, he was a happy dog. He lived in a comfy home with a large grassy yard, along with two people who loved him and six other dogs who were his best friends. In fact, Woody wasn't the only blind dog in his family. There were also Stanley and Porkchop (who, by the way, have their *own* book!). Even though these three blind dogs occasionally bumped into furniture, tripped over shoes, ran into walls and collided with the other dogs, they were all very content.

Woody hadn't always been so lucky. When he was about four years old, he found himself without a home or a family, abandoned in a crowded and noisy animal shelter. Word spread quickly about Woody's plight and he was soon adopted, traveling a long way to his new forever home.

After arriving, Woody was a bit overwhelmed. There seemed to be barking dogs everywhere, intruding furniture at every turn, and the layout of the house was a complete mystery. But, as was his nature, Woody learned quickly. Within a week, Woody had memorized the inside and outside of his new home. He could locate his food and water dishes, jump in and out of a car, walk on a leash and find all the doggie doors!

Woody knew precisely where his favorite napping places were and he recognized his family members by their voices, smell and feel. Most importantly, he also could hear the slightest movement of the treat jar!

As the days, weeks and months went by, Woody couldn't believe how fortunate he was. He had toys, bones, dog biscuits, car rides, friends and safety. There were kind people to pet him and good food to eat. He could lie in the sun, dig in the dirt and sleep on the bed. Having been blind since he was born, Woody didn't know what people, dogs or *anything* looked like. But, that didn't matter to Woody. He was loved and he was happy.

Unlike Woody, many blind dogs are unable to find good homes because they are viewed as helpless and needing constant supervision. Nothing could be further from the truth!

Woody was blind, but he was also a capable and confident dog. He was always ready to meet each day's challenges and learn from his mistakes. Perhaps more people might consider adopting blind dogs if only they could meet dogs like Woody!

And that is exactly what happened! Woody was named Goodwill Ambassador for Tootsie's Vision, the local group that had rescued him and many other blind dogs. As ambassador, Woody visited schools, community meetings, social events and book signings. He got to meet many people and he showed them how loyal, adaptable and lovable blind dogs could be!

One day, it was decided that Woody should become a candidate for Pet Mayor of the village in which he lived, a place called Corrales. Woody, of course, didn't understand what it meant to run for Pet Mayor, but since it would involve riding in the car, going to many new places and meeting even more people, he was all for it! Woody was also provided a snappy new vest with large letters stating that he was running for Mayor and he got to wear a lucky Snoopy tie around his neck.

Soon, Woody became a very busy dog. He greeted villagers on Sunday mornings at the Corrales Growers' Market, where many people stopped to say hello. Woody also appeared at local businesses and one restaurant even named a menu item after him....the *Woody burger*!

But Woody wasn't Pet Mayor yet. There were several other animals also running for the position.

One contender was Cooper the Pooper, a pretty orange hen who was often pulled along in a brightly decorated cart. Cooper was friendly and happy and always surrounded by her human family. She was also, as her name suggested, quite a pooper!

Hamilton was the only pig in the race. The size of a small dog, Hamilton had a flat nose, pointed ears and a curly little tail. He liked being pushed around in a modified baby stroller, into which he fit perfectly. Hamilton enjoyed having his prickly pink skin scratched by well-wishers and he welcomed offerings of apple slices with a contented "oink."

Also running for Pet Mayor was a large and handsome German Shepherd dog named Jake, who went by the odd nickname "Jake the Snake." Jake loved being with his family, but it was clear he didn't warm up easily to strangers or enjoy crowds. Sometimes, at a busy and noisy campaign event, Jake would pull his family away from the excitement, hoping to be taken home. And boy, could Jake pull!

Rosemary the Rooster was the name of the fifth contestant and Rosemary, despite having a girl's name, was most definitely a boy! Rosemary was tall and handsome, with long shiny feathers and a red crown of soft wavy flesh on the top of his head. When he crowed, Rosemary got everyone's attention.

Other than Jake, who was also a dog, Woody didn't' know what to make of these strange creatures. They smelled and sounded different than anything he had encountered before. But the more he hung out with them, the more he liked them.

As Woody continued to campaign all around Corrales, villagers began to recognize him and call out his name. "*Hey, Woody!*" they would shout, "*We voted for you!*" At first, dozens of people got to know Woody. Weeks later, it seemed like hundreds!

Curious people would often ask about Woody's blindness and how it affected him. They were amazed that, while Woody couldn't see them, he enjoyed their voices and welcomed their touch. When someone expressed sympathy because Woody was blind, Woody would often look up at the speaker and offer a wide toothy grin, showing them that he was a very contented dog and that there was no reason to feel sorry for him. It soon became clear to everyone who met Woody that his blindness did not interfere with his happiness one bit.

After each campaign event, contented but tired, Woody would eagerly head home, to the welcoming muzzles of Stanley and Porkchop, as well as Alex Marie, Lupe, Ozzie and Ziggy.

The busy weeks of campaigning went by quickly. Then, one sunny mid-October day, it was time to announce the winner of the Corrales Pet Mayor contest. Woody, Hamilton, Cooper, Jake and Rosemary gathered and waited together below a bandstand, anxious to find out who would win this important race.

The first name to be called was Jake, who, while not elected Pet Mayor, was named the honorary Village Police Chief for the next year; a perfect job for a large powerful dog!

Then Rosemary's name rang out and she was appointed as the Village Judge. One could easily imagine Rosemary sitting high atop a judge's bench, with everyone admiring his handsome red comb.

The Village Assessor's position was next, and it went to Hamilton the pig, who grunted his approval. He didn't know what an assessor was or did, but Hamilton was just happy that he could continue to ride around in his cart and eat apple slices.

Finally, only Cooper and Woody were left. One would become the Village Treasurer and the other the Pet Mayor of Corrales. A silence fell on the crowd as the announcement was read.

"The new Village Treasurer issssssssssss....*Cooper!* Cooper promptly celebrated by pooping.

That meant that Woody had WON! A cheer welled up. As the newly elected Pet Mayor of Corrales, Woody cautiously climbed the stairs to the stage and received his certificate, gifts and congratulations. He tilted his head, listening curiously to the clapping all around him.

The human mayor of Corrales rubbed Woody's head and, after that, Woody received many more pets, pats, ear scratches and belly rubs from his new constituents. He was in heaven!

Now, with his year as Pet Mayor of Corrales before him, Woody looked forward to meeting many more people and makings lots of new friends. It would be a wonderful adventure. And Woody could now show the world that blind dogs can do truly amazing things!!

WOODY

www.ingramcontent.com/pod-product-compliance
Lightning Source LLC
Chambersburg PA
CBHW061931290426
44113CB00024B/2878